Mighty Mach...

DUMP TRU
and oth...
BIG MACH

Ian Graham

QEB Publishing

QEB

Copyright © QEB Publishing, Inc. 2008

Published in the United States by
QEB Publishing, Inc.
3 Wrigley, Suite A
Irvine, CA 92618

www.qed-publishing.co.uk

Library of Congress Control Number: 2008010028

ISBN 978 1 60992 362 4

Printed in China

Author Ian Graham
Designers Phil and Traci Morash
Editor Paul Manning
Picture Researcher Claudia Tate

Picture credits (t = top, b = bottom, FC = front cover)

Alamy Justin Kase 5t, South West Images Scotland 17t
Corbis Construction Photography 21
JCB 8, 11t
Hochtief Aktiengesellchaft 20b
Komatsu 14, 15
Shutterstock Alexander Briel Perez FC, Bjorn Heller 1,
nialat 4, Zygalski Krzysztof 6, ownway 6b, Brad Whitsitt 7t,
Ljupco Smokovski 10, Mark Atkins 12, Florin C 13t,
Kamil Sobócki 16, Mark Atkins 18, Stanislav Komogorov 19a
Volvo 9t

Words in **bold** can be found in the glossary on page 23.

Contents

What is a dump truck?

Dump **trucks**, diggers, loaders, and bulldozers are all types of **construction** vehicles. These big machines help to build roads, bridges, tunnels, and tall buildings.

Some construction vehicles carry materials for building. Others have tools for digging, lifting, and pushing.

785B

24

These two diggers are being carried to work on the back of a transporter.

The huge back section of this dump truck can carry up to 150 tons (136 tonnes) of dirt and rubble.

Diggers

Digging machines, or excavators, work by pushing a metal **bucket** into the ground so that it fills up with dirt.

digging bucket

In one day, the biggest excavator in the world can dig a hole that is 60 feet (18 meters) deep!

Big metal teeth on the front of the digging bucket help to break up the ground.

This vehicle is a **backhoe**. It has a bucket in the back for digging and legs to keep it steady.

driver's cab

Some excavators have **tracks** instead of wheels. Tracks spread the weight and stop the excavator from sinking into soft ground.

tracks

Trucks

Before building work can begin on a **construction site**, huge piles of dirt and rubble may need to be shifted. Dump trucks and tipper trucks do this work.

Big trucks also deliver sand, gravel, bricks, and other building materials to the construction site.

A tipper truck tips up at the back to empty its load onto the ground.

Loaders

It would take a long time to fill a dump truck by hand! A machine called a loader can do the job much more quickly.

Smaller loaders are useful for working in awkward spaces.

A loader scoops up dirt in a big, wide bucket. Then the bucket is lifted up over a truck and the dirt is tipped into it.

As well as filling trucks, a loader's powerful arms can push dirt and rubble along the ground like a bulldozer.

Concrete mixers

Construction work needs a lot of **concrete**. Concrete is made by mixing sand, stones, and cement with water. Once the sloppy mixture has been poured, it sets as hard as a rock.

The drum of a mixer truck holds 20 tons (18 tonnes) of concrete—the weight of 12 midsized family cars!

drum

Concrete is brought to construction sites by mixer trucks. The concrete is carried in a big drum, which keeps turning to stop the cement from setting hard.

chute

On this mixer truck, the drum is emptied by pouring the concrete down a chute in the back.

Bulldozers

Bulldozers are big, powerful machines that are used to move dirt and rubble. A blade at the front of a bulldozer scrapes up the dirt and pushes it along in front.

blade

Bulldozers are used to clear the land to make it ready for building. They can flatten a big area very quickly.

Tracks help a bulldozer to grip the ground, so they can push hard.

tracks

Cranes on wheels

If a tall building is being constructed, materials and other heavy loads may have to be lifted high above the ground.

The **boom** is lowered when the crane is moving.

boom

On big construction sites, tall cranes are kept busy all the time. On smaller sites, special **mobile** cranes are brought in when they are needed.

Strong legs called **outriggers** stop the crane from tipping over.

outrigger

Roadbuilders

Before a road can be built, the ground has to be made very flat. Bulldozers and machines called scrapers and graders are used to flatten the area.

A grader scrapes a blade along the ground to smooth out the bumps.